THE full LIFE

A COMPANION JOURNAL FOR
FULL: FOOD, JESUS, AND THE BATTLE FOR SATISFACTION

Asheritah Ciuciu

ONE THING ALONE

Journal and layout design by Trew Studio

getting started

I don't know about you, but I have a stack of books on my nightstand, and the pile keeps growing. Even though I may have found a golden nugget or two in those pages, I'm so busy with other things that I rarely get to finish the books or apply what I'm learning.

I don't want that to happen to you.

So I teamed up with my friend Melissa to create this companion journal, to give you a place to jot down ideas, questions, and applications as you're reading my book *Full: Food, Jesus, and the Battle for Satisfaction*. Each week corresponds to a chapter in the book, and the quotes we've included will inspire you to experience The Full Life Jesus promises us.

Here are some journaling ideas to help you make the most of this companion journal:

> • **Write freely and authentically.** You can misspell words and write run-on sentences (your high school English teacher will never know.) Resist the urge to censor yourself; simply let your thoughts and feelings spill onto the page.

- **Jot down quotes that resonate with you,** and then reflect on what emotions or memories they trigger.
- **Consider answering the "Digest the Truth" questions** at the end of the chapters in Full. You'll also find reflection questions at the end of each week in this companion journal that will often prompt new discoveries.
- **Record your prayers as a letter to God,** processing what you're reading in conversation with Him.
- **Dare to ask yourself hard questions.** It's okay if you don't know the answer. This journey is a process that lasts a lifetime, and God will guide you every step of the way.

You'll find even more resources mentioned throughout the book—little incentives to help you not just read the chapters but apply them as well. You can access those at www.thefull.life.

As we begin this journey together, I pray that you would be awakened to the surpassing sweetness of Jesus. May you discover the fullness that He came to bring you in every area of your life.

Welcome to The Full Life!

week one

Knowing That Calories Aren't the Enemy

*"I have come that they may have
life, and have it to the full."*
John 10:10

One

I am so excited that you've chosen to begin this journey toward The Full Life in Jesus! When I first began my own journey, I never could have imagined the beautiful ways Jesus would reveal Himself to me:

- He cares about my struggles with food
- He welcomes me to be honest about what's really going on
- He longs to satisfy my deepest needs with Himself

It's easy to place our hope in the newest diet or miracle food, but the truth is that until we deal with the heart issues of seeking fullness in food instead of God, our eating habits will never change.

As we begin this journey together, receive this passage as a personal invitation from God to you:

> *Come, all you who are thirsty, come to the waters; and you who have no money, come, buy and eat! Come, buy wine and milk without money and without cost. Why spend money on what is not bread, and your labor on what does not satisfy? Listen, listen to me, and eat what is good, and your soul will delight in the richest of fare.*
>
> *Isaiah 55:1–2*

The freeing truth is that delicious food is not our enemy—it was God's idea in the first place. Let's abandon our self-constructed salvation projects and turn to Him instead, finding our soul's delight in the best this world has to offer: God Himself.

Why does God allow us to spend so much of life in the heat of battle?
Because He *never* meant for us to sip His Spirit like a proper cup of tea.
He meant for us to hold our sweating heads over the fountain
and lap up His life with *unquenchable* thirst.

BETH MOORE

Now choose life, so that you
and your children may *live*
and that you may love the Lord
your God, *listen* to His voice,
and hold fast to Him.
For the Lord is your *life*...

DEUTERONOMY 30:19-20

You are not your own;
you were bought at a *price*.
Therefore, honor God
with your *body*.

1 CORINTHIANS 6:19-20 (NLT)

You have made us for *yourself*,
Lord, and our hearts are restless
until they find *rest* in You.

———— 🍎 ————

ST. AUGUSTINE OF HIPPO

With *promises* like this to pull us on, dear friends, let's make a clean break with *everything* that defiles or distracts us, both within and without. Let's make our entire lives fit and holy *temples* for the worship of God.

— ❦ —

2 CORINTHIANS 7:1 (MSG)

If the idea of food as an *idol* seems strange to you, ask yourself if any of the statements below are true of you:

1. I could *never* give up my favorite food.

2. I spend more time and energy thinking about *food* than I do growing in my relationship with Christ.

3. I find more delight and *happiness* in food than in my relationship with Christ.

———— 🍓 ————

LESLIE LUDY

May your spirit, soul, & *body* be kept blameless at the
coming of our Lord Jesus Christ.

1 THESSALONIANS 5:23

We offer our *bodies* to God as part of what it means to *worship* Him.

———————————— ❦ ————————————

ROMANS 12:1

What stood out to you in this week's reading?

_____

_____

_____

_____

_____

_____

_____

_____

What new truth did you learn about God this week?

_____

_____

_____

_____

_____

_____

_____

What did you learn about yourself this week?

How can you apply these truths to live The Full Life?

Each of you should learn to *control* your own body.

1 THESSALONIANS 4:4

week two

Dressing for Success

Therefore, put on the full armor of God.
Ephesians 6:13

For the longest time, I searched for physical or mental solutions to my food fixation: a new healthy eating plan, a different exercise regimen, or a script of positive affirmations to give me super-human strength to resist those scrumptious cake pops.

But on my journey toward The Full Life, I discovered that God created us as three-personed beings—body, soul, and spirit—and until we address our food fixation on all three levels, we'll inevitably fail. There's spiritual work to be done here.

Scripture tells us that we have a very real enemy who has come to steal, kill, and destroy, and we'd be foolish to think our food struggles are somehow immune to this spiritual battle waging for our souls. But in His goodness, God has given us divine power and spiritual resources to win this battle.

God turned this area of shame and despair into a story of redemption and beauty. May you experience that transformation in your own life as well.

Finally, be *strong* in the Lord and in His mighty power. Put on the full armor of God so that you can *stand* against the devil's schemes.

 EPHESIANS 6:10-11

The desire God created in
each one of us to *connect* with
Him [is] an intense longing that
only the passionate *pursuit*
of Him can satisfy.

KATHY HOWARD

Eating habits become *sinful* when the habitual practice of them places us in bondage again—a *bondage* to sin from which Christ died to free us.

ELYSE FITZPATRICK

For though we live in the world, we do not wage *war*, as the world does. The weapons we fight with are not the weapons of the world. On the contrary, they have divine *power* to demolish strongholds.

———— ❦ ————

2 CORINTHIANS 10:3-4

It is not the yoke but the *resistance* to the yoke that makes the difficulty; the whole-hearted surrender . . . finds and secures the *rest*.

ANDREW MURRAY

Walk and live [habitually] in the [Holy] Spirit [responsive to and controlled and *guided* by the Spirit]; then you will certainly not *gratify* the cravings and desires of the flesh.

———— ❦ ————

GALATIANS 5:16 (AMPC)

One day, my child, you will have a new body and will no longer battle cravings in your flesh. Until then, know that *victory* is found not by fleeing the battle but by standing firm in the heat of the battle. I will fight for you; you need only to stand firm and be *still*.

PAGES FROM THE AUTHOR'S JOURNAL

God could fight [your addiction] all alone. He really doesn't need your help; however, God reserves the right to involve us in our own *victories*, so get ready to fight. Overcoming addiction may be the battle of your life. But it will also be the most rewarding, *liberating* victory of your life. It will be your own Goliath story for the rest of your days.

BETH MOORE

A woman is a *slave* to whatever has mastered her.

❦

2 PETER 2:19 (AUTHOR'S PARAPHRASE)

What stood out to you in this week's reading?

What new truth did you learn about God this week?

What did you learn about yourself this week?

How can you apply these truths to live The Full Life?

Discipline, for a Christian, begins with the *body*.

ELISABETH ELLIOT

week three

Choosing Truth Over Lies

You will know the truth, and the truth will set you free.
John 8:32

three

All day long there's a script that plays in our minds. We're often unaware of it, but it's there nonetheless. In fact, the more deeply engrained it is, the more difficult it is to discern the words.

As I journeyed toward spiritual fullness, I discovered that the greatest food battles were fought in my mind, as I identified subconscious lies that dictated my actions. But as I pinpointed those thoughts, I was able to later recognize them, take them captive, and replace them with God's truth.

The only way to take down the stronghold of food fixation is to knock down any thought patterns that stands in opposition to God's Word and to replace them with His Truth. So we:

- Dig up the lie,
- Fill up with Scriptural truth, and
- Grow up in mature faith

May your heart and mind be enlighted by God's Spirit to recognize these thoughts, and may you be filled to overflowing with the truth of His Word as it spills out into your words and actions, both in your eating and in every other area of your life.

We *demolish* arguments and every pretension that
sets itself up against theknowledge of God, and we
take captive every thought to make it *obedient* to Christ.

2 CORINTHIANS 10:5

_____

_____

_____

_____

_____

_____

_____

_____

_____

_____

_____

_____

_____

Making Jesus *enough* in
your life opens your eyes to
the way He sees the world.
And it *changes* you.

KRISTEN WELCH

You *alone* know the
human heart... .

———————◆———————

2 CHRONICLES 6:30b

Along with praying that God would enable to you *understand* what your particular areas of temptation are, you'll want to pray that you would be kept *alert* when they are present so you don't *succumb* to them.

ELYSE FITZPATRICK

search me, o God, and know my heart. Test me and know my anxious thoughts. See if there is any offensive way in me and lead me in the way everlasting.

PSALM 139:23-24

Comrades in this solemn fight. . .
Let us settle it as something that
cannot be *shaken*: we are here to
live holy, loving, lowly lives. We
cannot do this unless we walk
very, very *close* to our Lord Jesus.
Anything that would hinder us
from the closest walk possible
to us till we see Him face to face
is *not* for us.

AMY CARMICHAEL

Blessed be the God and Father of our Lord Jesus Christ, the Father of *Mercies* and God of all comfort, who comforts us in all our affliction, so that we may be able to *comfort* those who are in any affliction, the comfort with which we ourselves are comforted by *God*.

2 CORINTHIANS 1:3-4

I am the *way*, the *truth*, and the *life*.

JOHN 14:6

Which lie(s) stood out to you in this week's reading?

_____

_____

_____

_____

_____

_____

_____

What new truth did you learn about God this week?

_____

_____

_____

_____

_____

_____

What did you learn about yourself this week?

How can you apply these truths to live The Full Life?

You will know the *truth*, and the truth will set you *free*.

JOHN 8:32

week four

Stirring Up a
Holy Hunger

Blessed are those who hunger and thirst for
righteousness, for they will be filled.
Matthew 5:6

One of the hardest points in my journey toward overcoming food fixation was coming face-to-face with my weak appetite for God. I had grown up in the church and had served God all my life, and I honestly loved Him to the best of my ability. But as I opened my heart to God's searching Spirit, I realized that the root of my food problem was, in fact, that I didn't really desire God as much as I thought I did.

I began praying:

> "Deeper, Lord. I want to go deeper with You. Do whatever it takes to shake me from this apathy, and stir up within me a hunger for You."

And in His own perfect time and way, God began answering that heartfelt prayer. The skies didn't part and my heart didn't flutter. It was a gradual, almost unnoticeable change. But day by day, God awakened within me a deeper hunger for Him, and He continues to satisfy me with Himself.

Dare to be honest, with God and yourself, about the state of your spiritual appetite. And if you find it wanting, boldly ask Him to stir it up and do whatever it takes to make you desire Him more.

He will answer. And your life will be forever changed.

Then Jesus declared, "I am the bread of *life*. He who comes to me will never go hungry, and he who believes in me will never be thirsty. [...] Your forefathers ate the manna in the desert, yet they died. But here is the *bread* that comes down from heaven, which a man may eat and not die. I am the living bread that came down from heaven. If anyone eats of this bread, he will live *forever*."

JOHN 6:35-50

I will be fully *satisfied* as with the richest of foods;
with singing lips my mouth will *praise* you.

PSALM 63:5

I call on you, my God, for you
will answer me; turn your ear to me
and hear my prayer. [...] I will
be *vindicated* and will see your
face; when I awake, I will be
satisfied with seeing your likeness.

PSALM 17:6, 15

Indeed, if we consider the unblushing *promises* of reward and the staggering nature of the rewards promised in the Gospels, it would seem that Our Lord finds our desires, not too strong, but too weak. We are half-hearted creatures, fooling about with drink and sex and ambition when *infinite* joy is offered us, like an ignorant child who wants to go on making mud pies in a slum because he cannot imagine what is meant by the offer of a holiday at the sea. We are far too *easily* pleased.

C. S. LEWIS

No one can come to me unless the *father* who sent me draws them.

JOHN 6:44

You make known to me the path
of life; in your presence there is
fullness of joy; at your right hand
pleasures forevermore.

———————— ● ————————

PSALM 16:11 (ESV)

The greatest *enemy* of hunger for God is not poison but apple pie. It is not the banquet of the wicked that dulls our appetite for heaven, but endless nibbling at the table of the *world* [...] The greatest adversary of love to God is not his enemies but His gifts. And the most *deadly* appetites are not for the poison of evil but for the simple pleasures of earth.

JOHN PIPER

You open your hand and *satisfy* the desires of *every* living thing.

PSALM 145:16

What stood out to you in this week's reading?

_____

_____

_____

_____

_____

_____

What new truth did you learn about God this week?

_____

_____

_____

_____

_____

_____

Do you hunger for God? What did you learn about your spiritual appetite this week?

_____

_____

_____

_____

_____

_____

Write a prayer below asking God to stir up a holy hunger in your life.

_____

_____

_____

_____

_____

Blessed are those who hunger and thirst for righteousness,
for they will be *satisfied*.

MATTHEW 5:6 (ESV)

week five

Experiencing the Power of Fasting

*Whom have I in heaven but you? And earth
has nothing I desire besides you. My flesh and
my heart may fail, but God is the strength
of my heart and my portion forever.*
Psalm 73:25–26

Fasting has the incredible ability to reveal what really controls our appetites and affections, and for most of us, the answer is disappointing. So it's easy to avoid this spiritual discipline and pretend it's reserved for the super-spiritual elite.

But in fact, fasting is a humble invitation for God's Spirit to upend our lives, casting out idols we have allowed to woo us with their promises of comfort, and reorienting us to the only source of lasting satisfaction.

As you consider adding this spiritual discipline into your life, know that fasting is not a magic pill. In itself, it cannot change us. It's God's Spirit who uses this means of grace to teach us that we were created to find satisfaction in Him alone.

As discussed in *Full*, fasting is highly personal and looks different from person to person. If you're considering a fast this week, ask God to show you what to fast from, for how long, and in what way. And more than anything, ask Him to transform this exercise into a spiritual discipline that opens you up to His work in your life.

I have learned to be *content* whatever the circumstances. I know what it is to be in need, and I know what it is to have plenty. I have learned the secret of being content in any and *every* situation, whether well fed or hungry, whether living in plenty or in want. I can do all this through him who gives me *strength*.

PHILIPPIANS 4:11-13

To fall in *love* with God is the
greatest of all romances; to seek him,
the greatest *adventure*; to find him,
the greatest human achievement.

———— ❦ ————

AUGUSTINE OF HIPPO

> Fasting gives glory to God when it is experienced as a *gift* from God, aimed at knowing and enjoying *more* of God.
>
> JOHN PIPER

Whom have I in heaven but *you*?
    And earth has nothing I desire besides you.
My flesh and my heart may fail,
    but God is the *strength* of my heart
and my portion forever.

———————— ❧ ————————

2 CORINTHIANS 10:3-4

More than any other discipline, fasting reveals the things that *control* us. This is a wonderful benefit to the true disciple who longs to be *transformed* into the image of Jesus Christ. We cover up what is inside us with food and other things.

ANDREW MURRAY

But he said to them, "I have food to eat that you know *nothing* about. [...] My food," said Jesus, "is to do the *will* of him who sent me and to finish his work."

JOHN 4:32-34

We fast from what we can see and
taste because we have tasted and seen
the *goodness* of the invisible and
infinite God — and are desperately
hungry for *more* of him.

DAVID MATHIS

[Fasting] can be a *devastating* experience at first. Will I find spiritual communion with God sweet enough, and hope in His promises deep enough, not just to cope, but to flourish and rejoice in him? Or will I *rationalize* away my need to fast and retreat to the medication of food? The apostle Paul said, "I will not be mastered by anything" (1 Corinthians 6:10). Fasting reveals the measure of food's *mastery* over us--or television or computers or whatever we submit to again and again to conceal the weakness of our hunger for God.

JOHN PIPER

You can never learn that Christ is all you *need* until Christ is all you *have*.

CORRIE TEN BOOM

What stood out to you in this week's reading?

What new truth did you learn about God this week?

What did you learn about yourself this week?

_____

_____

_____

_____

_____

_____

_____

How can you begin fasting to experience The Full Life?

_____

_____

_____

_____

_____

_____

_____

Man does not live on *bread* alone, but on every *word*
that comes from the mouth of God.

MATTHEW 4:4

week six

Feasting on God's Word

How sweet are your words to my taste,
sweeter than honey to my mouth!
Psalm 119:103

It's easy to say, "God created us to find our satisfaction in Him." But how exactly does that happen, when God is invisible, untouchable, and incomprehensible?

The answer, as you've come to expect, is found in God's Word.

For too many of us, the Bible has become an academic text to be studied occasionally, whenever we need an encouraging word or some direction in our lives.

But far from being an instruction manual or a collection of positive quips, the Bible reveals the character of God through beautiful stories of personal redemption. In other words, we read the Bible to grow in our love and knowledge of God, and the more we feast on Scripture, the more His Spirit transforms our lives to reflect His.

Jesus Himself exemplifies a life that is saturated with God's Word, and He teaches us that we do not live by bread alone, but by every word that comes from the mouth of God (Matthew 4:4).

As you begin incorporating this spiritual discipline of feasting on the Word of God, may you come to discover, with the psalmist, that His Words truly are sweeter than the sweetest treat you'll find in a bakery.

When we eat a good meal, we *forget* about it in 24 hours; but when the Lord feeds us his Word, we have food for our souls that lasts *forever*.

Jim Cymbala

I have hidden your word
in my *heart* that I might not
sin against you.

PSALM 119:11

No *bible*, no breakfast.

LELAND WANG

I will tell you what *rule* I observed... when I was young, and too much addicted to childish diversions, which was this - never to spend more time in mere *recreation* in one day than I spend in private religious *devotions*.

SUSANNA WESLEY

Satisfy us in the morning
with your *unfailing* love,
that we may sing for joy and
be *glad* all our days.

PSALM 90:14

God's Word is a *good* use
of your time - you never
have to worry about wasting
your time if it's being spent
reading God's good and
useful and helpful Word.

ELIZABETH GEORGE

In joy and sorrow, in health and in sickness, in poverty and in riches, in *every* condition of life, God has [something] stored up in His Word for *you*.

D. L. MOODY

How sweet are your *words* to my taste, sweeter than *honey* to my mouth!

———————————————— 🍎 ————————————————

PSALM 119:103

What stood out to you in this week's reading?

_____

_____

_____

_____

_____

_____

_____

What new truth did you learn about God this week?

_____

_____

_____

_____

_____

_____

_____

What did you learn about yourself this week?

How can you begin feasting on God's Word in your life?

The heart cannot *love* what the mind does not *know*.

JEN WILKIN

week seven

Discovering Your
Triggers

Satisfy us in the morning with your unfailing love,
that we may sing for joy and be glad all our days.
Psalm 90:14

seven

A lone chocolate chip cookie in the coffee shop display case may seem innocent. And in fact, it is innocent. No food is off limits when we're filled and controlled by the Spirit of God.

But for many of us, encountering that cookie at the wrong time or place may trigger a reversion to old eating habits, whether it's emotional eating, guilt-tripping, or food obsessing. We don't like to think of food as an idol, but when we begin to believe that we need a certain food to be satisfied, it can quickly become that.

The truth is that the only thing we need is God Himself. And He is enough.

So we ask God to satisfy us with Himself every morning that we may release food to its proper place, resisting the urge to seek comfort in what will never satisfy.

As you encounter triggers throughout your day, may you become increasingly aware of God's surpassing satisfaction, and may your soul be wooed from the empty pleasures this world offers as you experience greater satisfaction in the presence of God.

If you don't feel strong *desires* for the manifestation of God, it is not because you have drunk deeply and are satisfied. It is because you have nibbled so long at the table of the world. Your soul is stuffed with small things, and there is no room for the *great*. God did not create you for this. There is an appetite for God. And it can be awakened.

JOHN PIPER

No temptation has overtaken you except what is common to man. And God is *faithful*; he will not let you be tempted beyond what you can bear. But when you are tempted, he will also *provide* a way out so that you can endure it. Therefore, my dear friends, flee from idolatry.

1 CORINTHIANS 10:13-14

Questions to gauge your
progress toward The *full* Life:

(1) Did I overeat this week
in any way?

(2) Did I eat in secret or out
of anger or frustration?

(3) Did I run to food instead
of God in any way?

(4) Do I believe that God is
pleased with me?

———————— ❧ ————————

INSPIRED BY KAREN EHMAN

Nothing *tastes* as good
as peace of mind *feels*.

LYSA TERKEURST

When Satan tempts me to despair and tells me of the guilt within
Upward I look and see Him there who made an *end* to all my sin.
Because the *sinless* Savior died, my sinful soul is counted free
For God, the just, is satisfied to look on Him and pardon *Me*.

TRADITIONAL HYMN

If we don't presently have an issue
that is actively *humbling* us, we veer
with disturbing velocity toward
arrogance & self-righteousness. We
are wise to remember that Christ
never resisted the *repentant* sinner.

—————— ◆ ——————

BETH MOORE

True conversion means *discipleship*, and further, that discipleship means *discipline*. We can experience great *freedom* when life's appetites serve God's kingdom rather than dominate our own lives.

BILL HULL

I have the *desire* to do what is good, but I cannot carry it out. For what I do is *not* the good I want to do *[that is, eat small portions; choose healthy options; stop when I'm full; and seek comfort in God, not food]*. No, the evil I do not want to do *[you know, overeating; mindless binging; eating junk food; choosing immediate, temporal satisfaction in my next bite; midnight pantry raids]*—*this* I keep on doing. Now if I do what I do not want to do, it is no longer I who do it, but it is sin living in me that does it. [...] Who will *rescue* me from this body of death? *[And here is where desperation sets in, and so the resolve to start a new diet or the retreat to another box of cookies. But...]* Thanks be to God—through Jesus Christ, our *Lord*.

ROMANS 7:18-25 (AUTHOR'S PARAPHRASE)

Taste and see that the Lord is *good*.

———————————— ❦ ————————————

PSALM 34:8

What stood out to you in this week's reading?

_____

_____

_____

_____

_____

_____

_____

What new truth did you learn about God this week?

_____

_____

_____

_____

_____

_____

What did you learn about yourself and your own triggers this week?

_____

_____

_____

_____

_____

_____

_____

How can you apply these truths to live The Full Life?

_____

_____

_____

_____

_____

_____

_____

Where the Spirit of the Lord is, there is *freedom*.

2 CORINTHIANS 3:17

week eight

Celebrating the Gift of Food

Everything God created is good, and nothing is to be rejected if it is received with thanksgiving, because it is consecrated by the word of God and prayer.
1 Timothy 4:4–5

It's so tempting to separate food into "good" and "bad" groups. You've likely read more than one article telling you to eat this and not that. And we certainly need to be wise in the way we nourish our bodies, so we ask God's Spirit to be our divine dietician, submitting to Him as He produces the fruit of self-control in our lives.

But let us not forget that we're are also free to enjoy the goodness of God's cornucopia of food.

Food is a good gift from a loving Father that is to be received with thanksgiving and worship. Let's stop calling evil what God has called good. This has been a turning point in my own journey toward The Full Life in Jesus, and He has freed me to enjoy His gift of food.

What if we turned our meal times into worship services, turning our hearts toward the Giver with gratefulness and praise?

With every bite and every meal, may we proclaim this beautiful truth:

"You open your hand and satisfy the desires of every living thing."

Psalm 145:16

What is the chief end of man? The chief end of man
is to *glorify* God, and to enjoy him *forever*.

THE SHORTER CATECHISM

Do not call anything impure
that God has made clean.

ACTS 10:15

But the *fruit* of the Spirit is love, joy,
peace, patience, kindness, goodness,
faithfulness, gentleness, and *self-control*.
Against such things there is no law.

———— ❧ ————

GALATIANS 5:22–23

Everything created by God is *good*,
and nothing is to be rejected
if it is received with gratitude;
for it is *sanctified* by means
of the word of God and *prayer*.

1 TIMOTHY 4:4–5 (NASB)

[Grace before meals] too often
denigrates into a mere form of words
—into lip service of the most heartless
form—and is too often looked
upon as a kind of religious charm.

———— ❧ ————

CHARLES JOHN ELLICOTT

Where there is no revelation, people cast off restraint; but *blessed* is the one who heeds wisdom's instruction.

PROVERBS 29:18

Blessed art thou, o Lord who feedest me from my youth, who givest food to all flesh: *fill* our hearts with joy and gladness, that we, having all sufficiency, may abound unto every good work in Christ Jesus our Lord, through whom glory, honor, and might be to thee *forever*. Amen.

TRADITIONAL BLESSING

So whether you eat or drink or *whatever* you do, do it all for the *glory* of God.

1 CORINTHIANS 10:31

What stood out to you in this week's reading?

_____

_____

_____

_____

_____

_____

_____

_____

_____

What new truth did you learn about God this week?

_____

_____

_____

_____

_____

_____

What did you learn about yourself (and about food) this week?

_____

_____

_____

_____

_____

_____

_____

How can you apply these truths to live The Full Life?

_____

_____

_____

_____

_____

_____

_____

Resist the devil and he will *flee* from you.

JAMES 4:7

week nine

Running to Win

Now to him who is able to do immeasurably more than all we ask or imagine, according to his power that is at work within us, to him be glory in the church and in Christ Jesus throughout all generations, for ever and ever! Amen.
Ephesians 3:20–21

nine

Too often our perfectionism hijacks our journey toward freedom from food fixation. Whether it's reaching for crackers instead of carrots during a movie night or ordering pizza instead of cooking a wholesome meal another night, our all-or-nothing mentality can make us think that one mistake means we've failed.

I know, because I've thought this way for far too long.

We try really hard to be perfect, but sooner or later we stumble and fall. So if we can't do it all, we don't do it at all.

But Jesus speaks into this flawed line of thinking to remind us that we can't be perfect on our own. That's the very reason He came into the world and died for our sins, offering forgiveness freely and unconditionally to all who believe in Him.

His forgiveness extends beyond salvation and into the stickiness and sloppiness of everyday life. Each day we have the opportunity to choose fullness in Jesus instead of turning to empty promises in our next bite. And every time we choose poorly, He stands ready and willing to give us a fresh start—no judgment, no condemnation, no shame. Just grace.

Pure, beautiful, abounding grace.

As you experience victories and defeats in your journey toward The Full Life, be reminded that His mercies are new every morning. May you rush to the throne of God and discover the forgiveness, freedom, and fullness He longs to give you.

> *"For we do not have a High Priest who is unable to empathize with our weaknesses, but we have one who has been tempted in every way, just as we are—yet he did not sin. Let us then approach God's throne of grace with confidence, so that we may receive mercy and find grace to help us in our time of need."*
>
> *Hebrews 4:15-16*

Truly I tell you, if anyone says to this mountain, 'Go, throw yourself into the sea,' and does not doubt in their heart but *believes* that what they say will happen, it will be done for them. Therefore I tell you, whatever you ask for in prayer, believe that you have received it, and it will be *yours*.

MARK 11:23-24

But those who hope in the LORD
will *renew* their strength.
They will soar on wings like eagles;
they will run and not grow weary,
they will walk and not be faint.

— ❦ —

ISAIAH 40:31

Whoever wants to be my disciple
must *deny* themselves, and take
up their cross daily and *follow* Me.

LUKE 9:23

As obedient children, do not *conform* to the evil desires you had when you lived in ignorance. But just as he who called you is holy, so be *holy* in all you do; for it is written: "Be holy, because I am holy."

1 PETER 1:14-16

Being set free and walking in
freedom are not the same. The
first was done for us by Jesus,
but the second we must *choose*
to do ourselves in His strength
and by His *grace*.

CHRISTINE CAINE

We eagerly await a Savior from [heaven], the Lord Jesus Christ, who, by the *power* that enables him to bring everything under his control, will transform our lowly bodies so that they will be like his *glorious* body.

PHILIPPIANS 3:20-21

Do you not know that in a race all the runners run, but only one gets the prize? Run in such a way as to get the prize. Everyone who competes in the games goes into strict training. They do it to get a crown that will not last, but we do it to get a crown that will last forever. Therefore I do not run like someone running aimlessly; I do not fight like a boxer beating the air. No, I strike a blow to my body and make it my slave so that after I have preached to others, I myself will not be disqualified for the prize.

1 CORINTHIANS 9:24-27

In all these things we are more than *conquerors* through him who *loved* us.

ROMANS 8:37

What stood out to you in this week's reading?

_____

_____

_____

_____

_____

_____

_____

What new truth did you learn about God this week?

_____

_____

_____

_____

_____

_____

What did you learn about yourself this week?

How can you apply these truths to live The Full Life?

Call on me in the day of trouble; I will *deliver* you, and you will *honor* me.

PSALM 50:15

week ten

Embracing the Grace of Community

Now you are the body of Christ,
and each one of you is a part of it.
1 Corinthians 12:27

God calls us to live life on earth with our eyes set on eternity. That perspective influences every aspect of life, from how we parent to how we love and even how we throw parties. But we don't have to figure this all out on our own.

Part of God's design for our lives includes placing us in communities of faith, surrounding us with women and men who love Him and sincerely desire to honor Him in their choices.

So as we walk toward the freedom and satisfaction Jesus offers, we can invite others to join us on our journey.

As you read this chapter, I pray that God will bring to mind people in your own faith community who can walk alongside you, study Scripture with you, feed the hungry with you, and celebrate victories with you.

But we ought always to thank God for you, brothers and sisters *loved* by the Lord, because God *chose* you as firstfruits to be saved through the sanctifying work of the Spirit and through belief in the *truth*.

2 THESSALONIANS 2:13

What blessed *relief* comes when we finally fall on our knees and humble ourselves before God. We suddenly realize what a heavy weight pride has been. It is exhausting to insist on thinking so highly of oneself with such mounting *evidence* to the contrary.

BETH MOORE

_____

_____

_____

_____

_____

_____

_____

_____

_____

_____

_____

This is the *confidence* we have in approaching God:
that if we ask anything according to his will, he *hears* us.

1 JOHN 5:14

In everything I did, I showed
you that by this kind of hard
work we must *help* the weak,
remembering the words the Lord
Jesus himself said: 'It is more
blessed to *give* than to receive.'

ACTS 20:35

God [created humans] so that
they would *seek* him and perhaps
reach out for him and *find* him,
though he is not far from any one
of us. 'For in *him* we live and
move and have our being.'

———— ❧ ————

ACTS 17:27-28

For the word of God is *alive* and *active*. Sharper than any double-edged sword, it *penetrates* even to dividing soul and spirit, joints and marrow; it judges the thoughts and attitudes of the *heart*.

HEBREWS 4:12

Let us then approach God's
throne of *grace* with confidence,
so that we may receive *Mercy*
and find grace to help us in our
time of *need*.

HEBREWS 4:16

I was hungry and you gave me something to *eat*.

MATTHEW 25:35

Do not get drunk on wine, which leads to debauchery.
Instead, be filled with the *spirit*.

———————————— ● ————————————

Ephesians 5:18

What stood out to you in this week's reading?

_____

_____

_____

_____

_____

_____

What new truth did you learn about God this week?

_____

_____

_____

_____

_____

_____

What did you learn about yourself this week?

_____

_____

_____

_____

_____

_____

_____

How can you invite your faith community into your journey toward The Full Life?

_____

_____

_____

_____

_____

_____

_____

So I say, walk by the *spirit*, and you will not gratify the desires of the *flesh*.

GALATIANS 5:16

week eleven

Serving with Food

Share with the Lord's people who are
in need. Practice hospitality.
Romans 12:13

eleven

Throughout Scripture, we see Jesus sitting down to meals with both the riffraff of society and the religious elite, and it's often over meals that dramatic life transformations took place. Just think of Zacchaeus, Mary of Bethany, and the 5,000 miraculously fed with five loaves and two fish.

Sharing a meal opens conversations and joins hearts. I can't help but think that this was intentional on God's part, as everything He does is intentional.

God has a beautiful way of redeeming the painful parts of our lives and using them for good, and this area of food is one of them. What has often been an isolating and embarrassing private struggle with food has become a door opener in my own life, as I've invited women both to sit at my table and to walk with me on this journey.

I hope you'll discover that food is a terrible master… but it can be a wonderful servant. We can use it to bridge language gaps when inviting foreigners into our homes. We can use it to communicate love to a hurting friend. We can use it to nurse a sick child back to health. And so much more.

As God continues to redeem the gift of food in your life, may you discover the many beautiful ways you can serve others with it as well.

The heart of *hospitality* is about creating space for someone to feel seen and heard and loved. It's about declaring your table a safe zone, a place of warmth and nourishment. Part of that, then, is *honoring* the way God made our bodies, and feeding them in the ways they need to be fed.

SHAUNA NIEQUIST

Whatever happens, conduct yourselves in a manner *worthy* of the gospel of Christ. Then, whether I come and see you or only hear about you in my absence, I will know that you stand *firm* in the one Spirit, striving together as one for the faith of the gospel [...] not looking to your own interests but each of you to the interests of the others.

Rejoice with those who rejoice; mourn with those who mourn.

Therefore *encourage* one another and build each other up, just as in fact you are doing. [...] And we urge you, brothers and sisters, warn those who are idle and disruptive, encourage the disheartened, help the weak, be *patient* with everyone. Make sure that nobody pays back wrong for wrong, but always strive to do what is *good* for each other & for everyone else.

PHILIPPIANS 1:27, 2:4; ROMANS 12:15; 1 THESSALONIANS 5:11-15

What people are *craving* isn't perfection. People aren't longing to be impressed; they're longing to feel like they're *home*. If you create a space full of love and character and creativity and soul, they'll take off their shoes and curl up with *gratitude* and rest.

SHAUNA NIEQUIST

Then Jesus said to his host,
"When you give a luncheon or
dinner, do not *invite* your friends,
your brothers or sisters, your
relatives, or your rich neighbors;
if you do, they may invite you
back and so you will be repaid.
But when you give a *banquet*,
invite the poor, the crippled,
the lame, the blind..."

LUKE 14:12-13

Love must be *sincere*. Hate what is evil; cling to what is good. Be devoted to one another in love. *Honor* one another above yourselves. [...] Share with the Lord's people who are in need. Practice hospitality. Bless those who persecute you; *bless* and do not curse. [...] Live in harmony with one another. Do not be proud, but be willing to associate with people of low position. Do not be conceited.

———————— ❦ ————————

ROMANS 12:9-16

Learn, little by little, meal by meal, to feed yourself and the people you *love*, because food is one of the ways we love each other, and the table is one of the most *sacred* places we gather.

SHAUNA NIEQUIST

See to it, brothers and sisters, that *none* of you has a sinful, unbelieving heart that turns away from the living God. But *encourage* one another daily, as long as it is called "Today," so that none of you may be hardened by sin's deceitfulness. We have come to *share* in Christ, if indeed we hold our original conviction firmly to the very end.

HEBREWS 3:12-14

So, if you *think* you are standing firm, be *careful* that you don't fall!

1 CORINTHIANS 10:12

What stood out to you in this week's reading?

_____

_____

_____

_____

_____

_____

What new truth did you learn about God this week?

_____

_____

_____

_____

_____

_____

_____

What did you learn about yourself this week?

_____

_____

_____

_____

_____

_____

_____

_____

How can you practice hospitality and help others discover The Full Life?

_____

_____

_____

_____

_____

_____

_____

They *devoted* themselves to [...] the breaking of bread and to *prayer*.

ACTS 2:42

week twelve

Navigating Seasons of Change

There is a time for everything, and a season for every activity under the heavens.
Ecclesiastes 3:1

twelve

All of life is a journey, and part of its beauty is the twists and turns that lead us to places we'd never expect.

But then again, part of life's greatest challenges are those very twists and turns. Just when you think you've got a handle on your new normal, something unexpected comes along and throws you off balance.

None of these unexpected changes catch God by surprise, and, in fact, when we look close enough, we can recognize His presence with us every step of the way. It's in this place of trying to navigate seasons of change that we learn to desperately cling to God, asking Him to walk with us all the way home.

As we foresee a bend in the road before us, we can spend time with the Lord and prayerfully ask Him to give us wisdom and discernment to adapt to this new season of our lives.

May every step of this journey, every new season, and every twist and turn bring you into a deepening relationship with God as you embrace The Full Life found in Jesus.

You, God, are my God,
    earnestly I seek you;
I thirst for you,
    my whole being *longs* for you,
in a dry and parched land
    where there is no water.
I have seen you in the sanctuary
    and beheld your power and your glory.
Because your love is *better* than life,
    my lips will glorify you.
I will praise you as long as I live,
    and in your name I will lift up my hands.
I will be fully *satisfied* as with the richest of foods;
    with singing lips my mouth will praise you.

PSALM 63:1-5

Prayer keeps us in *constant* communion with God, which is the goal of our entire believing lives. Without a doubt, prayerless lives are powerless lives, and prayerful lives are *powerful* lives; but believe it or not, the ultimate goal God has for us is not power but personal *intimacy* with Him.

BETH MOORE

If I take the wings of dawn, if I dwell
in the *remotest* part of the sea,
even *there* Your hand will lead me,
and Your right hand will lay hold of me.

PSALM 139:9-10 (ESV)

Even though I walk
   through the darkest valley,
I will fear no evil,
   for you are *with* me;
your rod and your staff,
   they *comfort* me.

PSALM 23:4

We can't overcome food
fixation on our own.
That *victory* belongs to God.
And He will *win* it.

———————— 🍎 ————————

PAGES FROM THE AUTHOR'S JOURNAL

Don't let your *happiness* depend
on something you may *lose*.

C.S. LEWIS

If you don't know what you're doing,
pray to the Father. He *loves* to help.
You'll get His help, and won't be
condescended to when you ask for it.
Ask *boldly*, believingly, without a
second thought

———— ● ————

JAMES 1:5-6 (MSG)

And the *peace* of God, which transcends all understanding, will
will guard your hearts and your minds in Christ Jesus.

PHILIPPIANS 4:7

In a loud voice they were saying: "*Worthy* is the Lamb, who was slain, to receive power and wealth and wisdom and strength and honor and glory and *praise*!"

———————————— ❧ ————————————

1 CORINTHIANS 15:33

What stood out to you in this week's reading?

_____

_____

_____

_____

_____

_____

_____

What new truth did you learn about God this week?

_____

_____

_____

_____

_____

_____

_____

What did you learn about yourself this week?

How can you apply these truths to live The Full Life?

He *raises* the poor from the dust, He *lifts* the needy from the ash heap
to make them sit with nobles, and inherit a seat of *honor*.

1 SAMUEL 2:8

about the author

Asheritah Ciuciu is the author of *Full: Food, Jesus, and the Battle for Satisfaction* and a popular blogger and speaker. She grew up in Romania as a missionary kid and studied English and Women's Ministry at Cedarville University in Ohio. Her passion is leading women deeper with Jesus through daily devotions and spiritual disciplines, both in her local church and around the world through digital discipleship. Asheritah is married to Flaviu, her childhood sweetheart, and together they raise their spunky children in northeast Ohio. Connect with her at www.OneThingAlone.com.

one thing alone

FINDING JOY IN JESUS

Connect with Asheritah
and get free resources to go deeper with Jesus:

www.onethingalone.com

- blog
- speaking events
- Scripture Art
- free ecourses
- online membership
- and so much more!

Free eCourse!

To say thank you for buying this book,
I'd like to give you an eCourse 100% free!

Enroll in *Quiet Time for Busy Women* today!
www.onethingalone.com/daily-devotions-ecourse

Made in the USA
San Bernardino, CA
28 January 2018